D1521348

creatures of the sea

Manatees

Kris Hirschmann

KIDHAVEN PRESS

An imprint of Thomson Gale, a part of The Thomson Corporation

Detroit • New York • San Francisco • San Diego
New Haven, Conn. • Waterville, Maine • London • Munich

THOMSON

GALE

For Steve P., best friend of the manatee.

For more information, contact
KidHaven Press
27500 Drake Rd.
Farmington Hills, MI 48331-3535
Or you can visit our Internet site at http://www.gale.com

LIBRARY OF CONGRESS CATALOGING-IN-PUBLICATION DATA

Hirschmann, Kris, 1967–
Manatees / by Kris Hirschmann.
p. cm. — (Creatures of the sea)
Includes bibliographical references and index.
Contents: Sea cows—Marine mammals—The manatee life cycle—
Staying alive.
ISBN 0-7377-3008-0 (hardcover : alk. paper)
1. Manatees—Juvenile literature. I. Title.
QL737.S63157 2005
599.55—dc22

2004029261

Printed in the United States of America

Table of Contents

Introduction

Legendary Beasts

Manatees are among the world's most recognized sea creatures. With their huge, gray bodies, rounded heads, whiskered snouts, and tiny black eyes, these animals are the subject of calendars, posters, TV documentaries, and more. It is possible to buy manatee magnets, cookies, stuffed toys, paperweights, and just about anything else imaginable. People everywhere love these animals for their calm, slow-moving ways.

But manatees were not always as popular as they are today. Just a few centuries ago, these animals were almost unknown. It is believed that ancient sailors sometimes spotted manatees. Not knowing what they were, the sailors mistook the manatees for half-human, half-fish creatures. The idea of the mermaid probably

A close-up look at a manatee shows its large, rounded head and short, stubby snout.

came from these early sightings. In fact, the scientific name of the order to which manatees belong is **Sirenia**. Commonly, these animals are referred to as **sirenians**. In ancient Greek mythology, sirens were mermaidlike beings that sang to confuse sailors and make them steer their ships into rocks.

It is strange that manatees are linked by name to creatures of death and destruction. Manatees are gentle animals that do not usually hurt other creatures, even when they are threatened. They depend on their sheer size for protection. For 50 million years, this has been enough. Today, though, manatees are in trouble. Once hunted nearly to extinction by humans, these creatures are now trying to make a comeback. But progress is slow. Manatees may be today's living legends, but there is no guarantee that they will be around to delight people in the future.

Sea Cows

At first glance, manatees may seem a little bit frightening. These creatures are so big that it seems as if they could harm a person very easily. But this would never happen. Manatees are gentle, fat, slow-moving grass eaters. Because of these traits, manatees are sometimes called "sea cows."

All manatees belong to the scientific family **Trichechidae**. This name comes from Greek words meaning "having hair." It probably refers to the manatee's prickly mustache. Because of this feature, scientists once believed that manatees were related to walruses, which have similar faces. But today scientists know that this is not true. Studies have shown that manatees and their cousins, the dugongs, are most closely related to elephants, aardvarks, and small rodents called hyraxes.

Types of Manatees

There are three types of manatees: West African, West Indian, and Amazonian. All of these manatee species need warm water to survive, so they are all found in shallow tropical and subtropical waters. Specific home areas or ranges, however, vary from species to species. The West African manatee, for example, is found only along the west coast of Africa. These animals can be seen along the shorelines of more than twenty countries, from Senegal in the north to Angola in the south.

West Indian manatees live on the opposite side of the Atlantic Ocean. These animals are divided into two subspecies: the Florida manatee and the Antillean manatee. The Florida manatee lives mostly along the east and west coasts of Florida but may range as far north as Virginia and as far west as Louisiana. The Antillean manatee is found throughout the Caribbean. These animals also live along the coasts of Central and South America from Mexico to Brazil. Sometimes they stray as far north as the Texas coast, although this is rare.

The Amazonian manatee is found only in South America's Amazon River, mostly in Brazil. It is the only type of manatee that never enters the ocean. The other species are able to survive in saltwater, brackish (partly salty) water, or freshwater, and often move back and forth between these environments. It is very common to see manatees in rivers, sometimes even far inland.

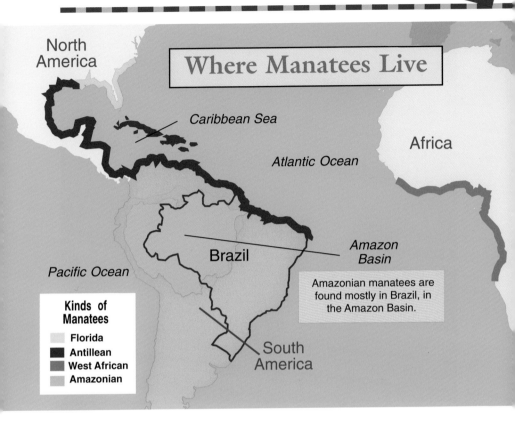

North America

Where Manatees Live

Caribbean Sea

Atlantic Ocean

Africa

Amazon Basin

Brazil

Pacific Ocean

Amazonian manatees are found mostly in Brazil, in the Amazon Basin.

Kinds of Manatees

Florida
Antillean
West African
Amazonian

South America

The Manatee Body

All types of manatees have one thing in common: They are big. The average length of a manatee is about 10 feet (3m), and the average weight is between 800 and 1,200 pounds (363 and 545kg). Some manatees are even larger. Really big individuals may be more than 13 feet (4m) long and may weigh as much as 3,500 pounds (1,589kg). Females are usually a bit larger than males.

The manatee's gigantic body begins with a rounded head. The head ends in a blunt snout that has hundreds of stiff hairs called **vibrissae**. Also located on the snout are two large nostrils and the

Two manatees at the Cincinnati Zoo nuzzle each other. Manatees are very gentle creatures.

manatee's mouth. Set back from the snout are two small, round eyes. Behind the eyes are two tiny pinholes that serve as the manatee's ear openings.

The manatee's head widens directly into a thick trunk without any sign of a neck. At the front and bottom of the trunk are two stubby **pectoral flippers**. Each of these flippers is tipped with three or four toenails. A manatee can control its pectoral flippers like arms. It uses these flippers for many things, including steering while swimming, pulling itself along the seafloor, digging, and bringing food to its mouth. Just behind the pectoral flippers, the trunk spreads out into a round, fat mass. It then tapers smoothly into a flat tail. The tail is broad and strong. A manatee waves its powerful tail up and down like a paddle to push itself forward through the water.

The manatee's tail, along with the rest of the body, is covered by leathery skin. The skin varies in color from grayish brown to black. The skin is constantly dying and falling off as the upper layer ages and is replaced by fresh, new skin. For this reason, manatees are often flaky and peeling all over.

Identifying Manatees

Although all manatees have some features in common, some differences make it possible to tell species apart. One way is by the skin. In the West African and West Indian species, the skin is rough

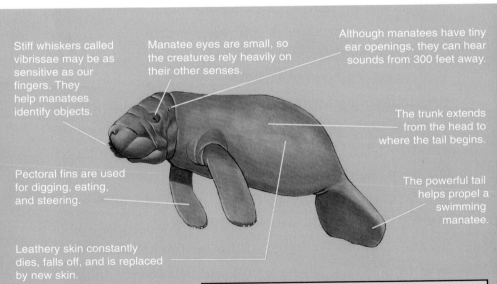

Stiff whiskers called vibrissae may be as sensitive as our fingers. They help manatees identify objects.

Manatee eyes are small, so the creatures rely heavily on their other senses.

Although manatees have tiny ear openings, they can hear sounds from 300 feet away.

The trunk extends from the head to where the tail begins.

Pectoral fins are used for digging, eating, and steering.

The powerful tail helps propel a swimming manatee.

Leathery skin constantly dies, falls off, and is replaced by new skin.

Physical Characteristics of the Manatee

and bumpy. In the Amazonian, the skin is smooth. Amazonian manatees also tend to be darker in color and often have blotchy pink patches on their bellies.

Size is another way to identify manatees. Amazonian manatees, for example, are usually a little bit smaller than their West African and West Indian relatives. They do not grow longer than about 9 feet (2.7m). Size can also be used to tell the sexes apart, since female manatees tend to be bigger than males. This identification method, however, is not always accurate. Instead, scientists look at a manatee's belly to figure out its sex. Females have reproductive openings near their tails, while males' openings are found in the middle of the belly.

Other Identifying Features

Some manatee features can be used to identify individuals rather than species or sex. The position and type of skin **parasites** is one such feature. Algae, barnacles, and other organisms often grow on a manatee's skin. The patterns the parasites form on the skin are unique to each manatee. These parasites move around constantly, so their arrangement cannot be used to track a manatee over long periods. But they are very useful in studies that last for days or weeks.

Permanent body and skin markings are more useful than parasites for identification. Especially in Florida, many manatees have scars on their backs and tails from collisions with motorboats. Scientists photograph the scars and use the photos to build manatee identification databases. These databases help scientists to recognize specific manatees year after year, wherever they may turn up.

Senses at Work

Manatees make their way through the world with the help of their senses. The most important sense to a manatee is probably hearing. Manatees have extremely sensitive ears and can detect very soft sounds. They often swim away if humans enter the water nearby, no matter how quietly they do so. The sound of a boat paddle can also send manatees fleeing. It is possible that manatees hear partly through their tiny ear openings, which lead to inner

Manatees munch on lettuce during feeding time at a rescue center. The manatee on the right has scars from a boat-propeller injury.

ear structures. But some scientists believe that manatees pick up sound vibrations mostly with an area near their cheekbones. Vibrations travel through the cheekbones to the inner ears, which then send sound messages to the brain.

Vision also helps manatees to get around. Manatees do not have great eyesight, but they see well enough to pick out major underwater features and even some things above the water's surface. Scientists believe that manatees can also see colors and adjust to changing light conditions. This means that, like humans, manatees see poorly at first in the dark. But after a few minutes, their eyes adjust and their vision improves.

Perhaps more useful in the manatee's environment is the sense of taste. Manatees often nibble on interesting objects and even each other. As they nibble they gather taste information. This information may help manatees identify each other. It may also help them stay healthy by avoiding bad-tasting, poisonous plants.

Touch is the last sense manatees depend on. Manatees have sensitive skin and spend some time every day rubbing themselves against rocks or logs. They can also "touch" things at a distance using the sensory hairs all over their backs. Water currents and disturbances move these hairs, letting a manatee know that objects or animals are nearby. It is a useful ability for a slow-moving creature. Even when it is sitting still, a manatee can gather all the information it needs to survive.

Marine Mammals

Even though manatees spend their lives in the water, they are not fish. They are **marine mammals**. This means that they breathe air, like land animals do. Manatees also keep a constant body temperature, like mammals. They do not get warmer or colder along with their surroundings, as most sea creatures do. These two needs—getting air and staying warm—are important to all mammals, and they guide a manatee's life.

Breathing

Because manatees need oxygen to survive, they always stay in the uppermost regions of the sea. These animals are rarely found deeper than 10 feet (3m) below the ocean surface. Dives of up to 33 feet (10m) occur once in a while, but these dives do not last long. Within minutes, a deep-diving manatee pops back up to get fresh air.

Manatees breathe through the two nostrils located on top of their snouts. The nostrils are covered with flaps of skin that open and close like trapdoors. The manatee tightly closes these flaps whenever it is below the sea surface to prevent water from entering. To breathe, the manatee pokes the tip of its snout out of the water and opens the flaps. It blows stale air out of its body and then sucks in a new breath of oxygen. This exchange process is very efficient. A manatee exchanges about 90 percent of the air in its lungs with each breath. In contrast, humans exchange only about 10 percent of their lung contents each time they breathe out and in.

Manatees usually breathe once every two to four minutes. But if necessary, a manatee can stay underwater for as long as twenty minutes. A manatee that gets trapped underwater for longer than this may run out of oxygen and suffocate, but it will not drown. Manatees do not breathe automatically, as humans do. They must purposely open their nose flaps to get air. So even if it is unconscious, a manatee's nose flaps will stay clamped tightly shut.

Floating and Sinking

After air enters a manatee's body, it passes into two large, long lungs. Each lung is about 3 feet (91cm)

A manatee pops its whiskered snout out of the water for a breath of air.

long. When they are full of air, these lungs act like balloons to keep a manatee's heavy body afloat.

A manatee does not want to float all the time, of course. It must also be able to sink. Otherwise, it would just bob at the sea surface all day long. To balance the **buoyancy** of their lungs, manatees have thick, heavy bones that help weigh them down. Manatees can also use their trunk muscles to squeeze the lungs into a smaller area. Doing this reduces the amount of air inside the manatee's body. In turn, this causes the manatee to have less upward lift. By using its muscles in this way, a manatee has control over its buoyancy. It can rise, sink, or hover in the water without moving its outer body parts at all.

Despite its enormous size, the manatee is a graceful swimmer, thanks to its powerful flippers and paddlelike tail.

Because they are so good at controlling their buoyancy, manatees are surprisingly agile swimmers. These creatures can do barrel rolls, swim on their backs, and stand head first or tail first in the water. Despite their bulk, manatees move with ease in their watery environment.

Warm-Weather Creatures

Temperature control is another important factor in a manatee's life. As mammals, manatees must maintain an internal body temperature of about 97.5°F

(36.4°C). Because manatees live in areas that are hot most of the time, their bodies are designed to keep cool. Manatees have very slow metabolisms, which means that they do not produce a lot of internal heat compared with other animals of the same size. They do have a layer of fat about 1 inch (2.5cm) thick beneath their skin, but this fat layer does not provide enough insulation to trap a lot of heat.

The manatee's body design works wonderfully during the summertime, when water temperatures are high. But keeping warm is not such a simple task during colder times of the year. Manatees start to feel chilly when water temperatures drop below about 68°F (20°C). If a manatee cannot find a

With a slow metabolism and efficient body design, the manatee maintains a comfortable body temperature even in warm water.

warmer spot, it gets sluggish and stops eating. It develops white patches and sores all over its body, and soon it dies of **exposure**.

Manatee deaths related to the cold sometimes happen in Florida. In 1977, 38 manatees in one small area perished from the cold. And during the winter of 1989–1990 at least 46 manatees died due to winter weather. Spells of unusually cold temperatures during these periods made it impossible for the manatees to stay warm.

Keeping Warm

To avoid freezing to death, most manatees **migrate** between summer and winter homes. During the hottest parts of the year, when both inland and ocean waters are warm, manatees can be found just about anywhere in their ranges. When the water temperature drops below a manatee's comfort zone, however, these animals head for warmer areas. They look for a warm, safe spot where they can spend the winter months comfortably.

More is known about the migration habits of the Florida manatee than any other species. In Florida many manatees head for inland springs, where the water temperature seldom drops below 72°F (22°C). Natural manatee gathering places include Blue Spring State Park, Crystal River Wildlife Refuge, and Homosassa Springs. Manatees may also spend the winter near power plants, which pump hot water into the environment. Plants in Cape Canaveral,

Snorkelers swim with a group of manatees at the Crystal River Wildlife Refuge, one of several manatee gathering places in Florida.

Fort Lauderdale, Fort Myers, Tampa Bay, and other areas attract up to 200 manatees apiece during cold weather.

In Florida the winter season ranges from about November to March. During this time manatees group together in warm places. They may swim into colder water during the daytime to find food, but they return each night to their winter resting place. They follow this pattern until spring arrives and the water warms up. Then the manatees leave their refuges and resume their wandering lifestyles. Until the weather turns cold once again, these gentle giants will roam freely in the oceans and rivers of the world.

chapter 3

The Manatee Life Cycle

M anatees have long lives. If conditions are good, a manatee may live up to 60 years. Scientists know this because manatees have growth patterns on their ear bones much like tree rings. Anytime a manatee's body is found, the ear bones are removed and studied to pinpoint the manatee's age at death.

During its lifetime, a manatee will come into contact with many other manatees. But it will not form any lifelong bonds. The only close relationships a manatee forms are with its mother or its offspring. And even these bonds are just temporary. Most of the time, manatees live solitary lives, depending only on themselves for survival.

Mating Time

Springtime is mating season for most manatees. At this time of the year, a female who is getting ready to mate gives off chemical signals. Males taste these drifting signals and swim toward the female. Depending on the number of manatees in the area, a female may draw quite a crowd. Up to twenty males have been seen gathering around a single female manatee.

Even when a female is in **estrus**, she will not mate until she is ready. She swims along, ignoring her many suitors. All of the males follow the female,

Females may mate with one or several males. Once pregnant, they usually carry just one calf.

waiting for the right moment. Because there are so many males, there is no guarantee that any one male will get to mate with the female. So all of the males push each other around as they swim. They try to stay as close as possible to the female, hoping to be in the best position to mate when the time comes. This struggle seems to bother the female, who twists and turns in the water as if trying to lose her would-be mates. Sometimes a female manatee even hauls her body out of the water and lies on dry land for a while to give herself a break from the constant attention.

When the female is finally ready, she mates with one or several males. Mating is done belly to belly and in a variety of positions. For example it can take place with both manatees hanging vertically in the water. Or the male can swim upside down beneath the female. After mating, the males swim away. They will not help in the female's pregnancy or with parenting duties.

A Calf Is Born

A pregnant female usually carries just one **calf**, although twins are sometimes seen. The calf grows inside the female's body for twelve to thirteen months. When it is time for the calf to be born, the female finds a quiet place where she can be alone. The baby manatee emerges from the birth canal, which is located on the female's belly near the tail. The calf may be born either head first or tail first.

Despite its rather large size, this newborn manatee calf feels safest close to its mother's side.

A newborn manatee calf looks tiny compared with its giant mother, but it is still big. Baby manatees can be anywhere from 2.5 to 4.5 feet (76 to 137cm) long and may weigh up to 70 pounds (32kg). Young manatees are much darker in color than adults when they are first born. After a few months, their skin slowly lightens until it reaches the typical color of their species.

Manatees know how to swim as soon as they are born. Once a calf emerges, it immediately moves upward to take its first breath of air. The mother may help her baby by pushing it with her snout, or the calf may make the trip entirely on its own. Either

A manatee nurses her twin calves. During their first year of life, calves get almost all of their nourishment from nursing.

way, the newborn soon reaches the water's surface. It will stay there for the first few hours of its life, popping its small nose out to breathe every twenty seconds or so. The mother manatee stays by her little one's side, making sure it is safe and content.

During this time, mother and baby call to each other constantly with squeals, squeaks, chirps, and grunts. This exchange lets the calf know that its mother is nearby. Some scientists also believe that this early conversation helps a calf bond with its mother.

Early Life

Within a few hours of its birth, a manatee calf begins to nurse. It drinks its mother's milk from teats found beneath the pectoral flippers. Even though the calf is born with teeth and will start nibbling on grasses within a few weeks, it depends mostly on its mother's milk for the first year of its life. At first the calf nurses for just a few seconds at a time. As the young manatee gets better at holding its breath, it will nurse for several minutes per session. By nursing often throughout

A baby manatee begins nursing soon after birth. As the calves learn to hold their breath, they can nurse for longer periods.

the day, the calf gets plenty of fat-rich milk that helps it grow quickly. Over the next few months, the little manatee will gain about 1 pound (0.45kg) every day.

Especially in the early days, a baby manatee stays close to its mother's side. It calls to its mother often, and the mother responds with high-pitched squeals. Every now and then the mother leaves her baby in a quiet place while she goes to look for food. But she always returns quickly to make sure her calf is safe.

During its first year, a manatee calf learns many things. For instance, it figures out how to act like a manatee by playing games like follow-the-leader and tag with its mother. It discovers what foods are good to eat and where they can be found. And perhaps most important, it learns the location of warm spots where it can spend the winter. Calves whose mothers die do not know where to go when cold weather arrives, so they may not survive their first year.

Growing Up

Sometime between one and two years of age, a manatee calf is weaned. This means it no longer drinks its mother's milk. The young manatee is ready to begin life on its own. At this point most manatees leave their mothers, although some stay nearby for several years. During this time the youngsters become bigger, stronger, and more independent. Like adults, they

A calf dozes at its mother's side in the grasses at the bottom of Crystal River, Florida.

live slow-moving, peaceful lives that involve a lot of eating and sleeping, along with a little curious exploration of the environment.

As time goes by, young manatees reach maturity and are able to have young of their own. Some females become mature when they are four or five years old, but seven or eight years is more typical. Males take a little longer, maturing around nine or ten years of age. Once this milestone is reached, the young manatees start to look for mates. Males will mate every year for the rest of their lives, while females will mate every two to three years. If all goes well, a female manatee will have a calf every three years throughout her adulthood.

Young adult manatees that have never been parents before may have trouble taking good care of their calves. But as female manatees get older, their mothering skills improve. For this reason, later-born calves have a better chance of survival than early calves. Any calves that live through their first year, however, are likely to make it to adulthood. They will eventually mate and have calves of their own, and the manatee cycle of life will continue.

4

Staying Alive

M anatees are **herbivores**, which means they eat only plants. They must eat a huge amount each day to get the nutrients they need. A manatee may eat 10 percent of its body weight— 100 pounds (45kg) or more—in food during a single day. It takes six to eight hours for a manatee to find and swallow all this plant matter.

Finding enough food to stay alive from day to day is not the only challenge manatees face. An even bigger challenge is the survival of the species. All manatee species are **endangered** or **threatened**. In 2004 scientists counted just 2,568 manatees in the waters of Florida. Populations of other species are low as well. It will take great care to keep today's manatee populations healthy and stable.

Finding Food

Manatees are not picky eaters. They will happily gobble down at least 60 kinds of plants. In Florida favorite manatee foods include sea grasses, mangrove leaves, algae, water hyacinths, and water hydrilla. Manatees in other regions eat different things, depending on what is found in their area. Amazonian manatees, for example, sometimes eat floating palm fruits.

Most manatees prefer to eat plants growing from the sea or river floor. A manatee may use its strong front flippers to pull these plants up by the roots. Or

An Amazon manatee swims in a river in Brazil. Manatee species throughout the world are threatened or endangered.

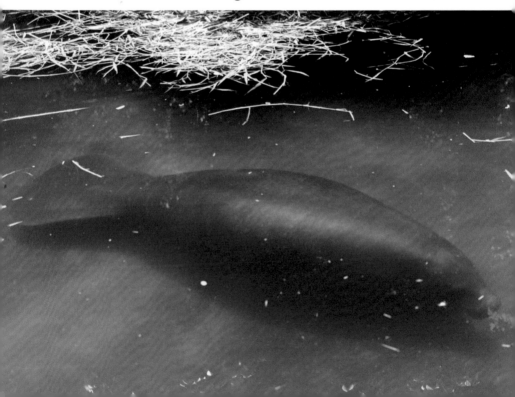

A large manatee licks the face of an underwater photographer. Manatees are curious creatures that often interact with humans.

it may leave the plants where they are and simply graze on the leaves. If bottom-growing plants are not available, a manatee may eat things that are floating in the middle of the water or on the water's surface. It may poke its head out of the water to nibble on hanging branches. Every now and then a manatee even beaches its massive body to eat grass or other plants growing along quiet shorelines.

Even though manatees are plant eaters, they often eat snails, worms, and other small creatures that cling to the vegetation they eat. Some scientists believe that the **protein** in these creatures' bodies is an important part of the manatee's diet. This idea is supported by the fact that captive manatees like to eat fish. In the wild, fishermen have seen manatees stealing fish from their nets. And one manatee was even seen eating a dead rat that had fallen into the water.

Food is not the only thing manatees need to stay alive. These animals also need freshwater for drinking. Manatees that live in saltwater environments often make trips to river mouths for this purpose. They may also drink from sewers and other freshwater outlets. Sometimes they even drink from garden hoses if no people are around.

Chewing and Digestion

Once a manatee has found food, it gets ready to eat. It uses its flexible lips and stiff, movable vibrissae to push food into its mouth. Once food enters the mouth, it is crushed with ridged pads at the front of the upper and lower jaws. The crushed food is then pushed backward by a large tongue.

In the rear of the mouth, the food is ground further by 24 to 32 large, lumpy molars. Because sea grasses and other manatee foods are rough and gritty, they wear these molars down over time. Manatees cope with this by continually replacing their teeth. The worn front teeth fall out and new ones slowly move forward to take their place. This conveyor-belt process guarantees that a manatee will be able to chew food throughout its lifetime.

After food has been thoroughly chewed, it moves into the manatee's stomach. The stomach coats the food in a thick layer of mucus. The slimy food then passes into the intestine, which may be as much as 130 feet (39.6m) long. Most of the digestive process is carried out in the intestine by special bacteria. The process is very slow, taking up to a week, and it produces huge amounts of methane gas. This gas bubbles out of the manatee's body through an opening near the tail. The same opening releases any solid waste materials that cannot be digested.

A manatee in Florida munches on water hyacinth, one of its favorite foods. Manatees are primarily plant eaters.

Manatees in Danger

Although manatees do a lot of eating, they have few natural enemies and are very rarely eaten themselves. West Indian and West African varieties are occasionally attacked by sharks, crocodiles, and alligators. Amazonian manatees may be killed by jaguars and caimans. But such attacks are rare. Manatees are so big that few animals will bother them.

This is not true of humans, though. In past centuries, humans hunted manatees for food, oil, and other uses. By the early 1900s this practice had greatly reduced the number of manatees around the world. One manatee species, the Steller's sea cow, was even hunted to extinction in the 1700s.

Although manatee hunting is now illegal in most places, human activities still take a toll on manatee populations. Despite laws that protect manatees, some people still hunt these animals for fun or for profit. Manatees may also die after being trapped in flood-control gates or navigation locks (mechanical devices that open and close to control the water flow in a river). Used fishing line and nets left in the water are also a danger to manatees, which may become entangled and eventually die.

The biggest problem for manatees today, however, is motorboat traffic. During migration periods, manatees often swim through areas where boats are common. Because manatees are slow moving and dark in color, they are hard to see.

A manatee swims dangerously close to a motorboat, which can cause injury or even death with its propellers.

Manatees are able to hear motorboats coming, and they can swim away at speeds of 15 miles (24k) per hour in an emergency. But manatees often hear motorboats too late to get out of the way. They are struck by the boats or slashed by their propellers. These manatees often die. Some lucky manatees survive, but they bear scars for the rest of their lives as a result of their motorboat encounters.

Protecting Manatees

Steps are being taken to protect manatees from humans. In Florida, for example, laws require boaters to slow down in marked manatee zones. Roped-off areas are created each year in manatee wintering spots to prevent curious people from getting too close to the animals. And rescue programs are in place to nurse sick or injured manatees back to health. These animals are then released back into the wild.

Manatees forage for food in the sand with their snouts. The future of these gentle giants depends on human efforts to protect them.

National and international laws also protect manatees. In the United States manatees are covered by the Marine Mammal Protection Act of 1972 and the Endangered Species Act of 1973. These acts make it illegal to hunt, capture, kill, or harass manatees. A person who does any of these things may be fined up to $20,000. Florida has an additional act, the Florida Manatee Sanctuary Act of 1978, that lays out guidelines for enforcing the laws. Similar laws protect manatees in other parts of the world.

Saving Manatees

Laws may not be enough to protect manatees if people do not understand the value of these creatures. For this reason, many organizations are trying to teach the public about manatees. One such group is the Save the Manatee Club, which was founded in 1981 by former Florida governor Bob Graham and singer Jimmy Buffett. The Save the Manatee Club is dedicated to raising money for manatee preservation. Funds from this organization's Adopt-a-Manatee program go toward public education projects, manatee research, rescue and rehabilitation efforts, and manatee habitat protection. Florida is also working to raise awareness with its "Save the Manatee" specialty automobile license plate. These plates feature the manatee's image along with the car's license number. The money made from sales of the plates goes toward manatee-related projects.

These efforts and others have made people very aware of the manatee's plight. They have also helped people realize that, despite their bulk, manatees are gentle creatures that need protection to survive in today's world. Providing this protection will take time and effort. But as long as people help manatees, there is hope that they will survive and thrive in the world's oceans for many, many years yet to come.

Glossary

buoyancy: Tending to rise or float in water.

calf: A young manatee.

endangered: Facing a high risk of extinction.

estrus: Readiness to mate.

exposure: Lack of protection from harmful elements, such as the cold.

herbivores: Animals that eat only plants.

marine mammals: Mammals that live in an ocean environment.

migrate: To move from one seasonal home to another.

parasites: Organisms that live in or feed on other living organisms.

pectoral flippers: Armlike flippers at the front and bottom of a manatee's body.

protein: A substance made by all cells. Proteins are essential for life.

Sirenia: The name of the scientific order to which manatees belong.

sirenians: Another name for manatees and dugongs.

threatened: Likely to become endangered in the near future.

Trichechidae: The name of the scientific family to which manatees belong.

vibrissae: The sensory hairs on a manatee's snout.

For Further Exploration

Books

Carol A. Amato, *Chessie, the Meandering Manatee.* Hauppage, NY: Barron's, 1997. While visiting their uncle in Florida, Carrie and Ben learn all about the manatee. Includes the true story of Chessie, a manatee that traveled to New York and back.

Laurie Halse Anderson, *Manatee Blues.* Milwaukee, WI: Gareth Stevens, 2003. This book is part of the "Wild at Heart" fiction series, which is about a group of young veterinary volunteers. In this installment, the kids have an adventure at a manatee rescue center.

Phyllis Perry, *Freshwater Giants: Hippopotamuses, River Dolphins, and Manatees.* New York: Franklin Watts, 1999. Includes information about manatees and other large animals that can be found in the world's rivers.

Web Sites

Homosassa Springs Wildlife Park (www.manatee cam.com). Tune in to the live Manatee Cam during winter months to see manatees in action.

Kids Only Manatees and Dugongs (www.cep. unep.org/kids/kids.html). General information about manatees and dugongs. Each page includes a manatee graphic to print out and color.

Save the Manatee Club (www.savethemanatee. org). Learn about manatees, adopt a manatee, and more.

Index

picture credits

about the author

Kris Hirschmann has written more than one hundred books for children. She is the president of the Wordshop, a business that provides a variety of writing and editorial services. She holds a bachelor's degree in psychology from Dartmouth College in Hanover, New Hampshire.

Hirschmann lives just outside Orlando, Florida, with her husband, Michael, and her daughters Nikki and Erika.